OUT OF THE WORLD

HYSTERICAL BOOOKS

OUT OF THE WORLD

POEMS

KRISTINE SNODGRASS

HYSTERICAL BOOOKS

2016

Copyright © Kristine Snodgrass 2016
All rights reserved under
International and Pan-American Copyright Conventions.

No portion of this book may be reproduced in any form without the written permission of the publisher, except by a reviewer, who may quote brief passages in connection with a review for a magazine or newspaper.

Cover Image: Emily Arwood

Author photograph: Michelle Benson Sweeney
Design, production: Jay Snodgrass
Library of Congress Cataloging-in-Publication Data
Out of the World by Kristine Snodgrass — First Edition
ISBN — 978-0-940821-03-3
Library of Congress Cataloging Card Number — 2015920006

Hysterical Books is dedicated to the publication and appreciation of fine poetry and other literary genres.

HYSTERICAL BOOKS
Email: hystericalbooks@gmail.com
Published in the United States by Hysterical Books
Hysterical Books is an imprint of Apalachee Press
Tallahassee, Florida • First Edition, 2016

for
Laika

Contents

air

Dog   3
Moscow, Before Sputnik   4
Susan is Fabulous   5
Hester's Room   6
Laika   7
Canine Astronomy Lesson   8
The Cage and the Animal   9
Hester's Wish   10
Dog   11

[annals: show]   12
[annals: concede]   13
[annals: rake]   14
[annals: tag]   15
[annals: foster]   16
[annals: catch]   17
[annals: lift]   18
[annals: evolve]   19
[annals: thrust]   20

The Hoohah   21
Foliation as Girl   22
Stampeding of Horses and Feet   23
Dr. Malashenkov   24
Albina & Mushka   26
Voices of the Airways   27

Horse Well   28
Horse Well   29
Horse Well   30
Horse Well   31
Horse Well   32

Semantics   33

breath

Re-memory of Water   36
Hester's Shoes   38
Some Women Marry Houses   39
Swimmer's Ear   40
Laika's Rendezvous   41
Mountains of Brie and Wiry Ocean   42
Dog   43
Hester's Rampage   44
Hester   45
Planet Hester   46
Star   47
Terrible   48
Cowpuncher   49

[annals: see]   50
[annals: crill]   51
[annals: oceans]   52
[annals: argent]   53
[annals: autosuggestion]   54

Guarantor   55
Average   56
Remarkable   57

Decidedly we are out of the world.

—Arthur Rimbaud, *A Season in Hell*

We can only pray in this time of aloneness and suffering that God will be merciful and speed the end. This voiceless cry of mercy, as this satellite spans the Earth, should be long remembered as the symbol of the torture the animal world must go through. And I don't mean to be facetious at all, but something to be remembered is that there is a female up there circling Mother Earth.

—Miss America, 1957.

Sputnik II carried the first dog in space, Laika.

air

Dog

Light as a carved piece of abalone, there is always someone knocking on my door, and you taught me to answer it. To let them in and serve them tea.

And when they are here, in this room, I have forgotten about the heart of my well. What we have created together remains an umbra.

Moscow, Before Sputnik

A man's voice bends me like a pine tonight—
Fluorescent it seems against the free stars
And as it gains near, the air turns white,
Turns inward, and freezes into milk bars.
Men gather around my head, start talking
In Russian, and gently lift me with beaks
So large I have room to roll around in
them, like pink, wet cavernous streets.

We are lifted, all of us, mice, horses
And wrens—the sky lights are soft blue tonight,
People everywhere are drinking goblets.
From your backyard, constellations have no
color; like silver eyes—
they are spools

                spinning lightly,

                              gathering threads.

Susan is Fabulous

But she is an alcoholic. I am trying to come to terms with this but there are too many movies that I have missed all year.

Sasha is bemoaning her job and no one looks forward to using a fresh ballpoint like I do.

There are so many addictions I want to tell Sadie about. The one her father has, the one her best friend has.

I want to scoop them all up ( ) into a voile sheet and bless them.

Bless you.

I will give them a list of the containments holding them in like geodesic domes.

( ) ( )

We are not always irradiant beings, Shar. We sit in light defused rooms and wait for the opening credits.

No previews please. Run, Sally, Run.

Hester's Room

There is a verby miscreant in my bedroom. She is a lilac sizzling on the desk. She sits solidly with no thoughts—and I admire her.

How do we rein in the petals? How do we paint lives with scrambled eggs and friends? There is a raisin that fell into that publisher's lap. It was supposed to be in some cereal, cookie, or dust pan. I want to put it in my mouth, suck the dryness from it. Evaporate myself.

There is no glitch in a fledgling starlet. She is not sending cloth diapers out. She is not making casseroles from gowns, and dying her hair gray and stringy.

        glockenspiel

Hold it up to the transfixed sun and hit. We are all writing Morse code.
- -....

        radiation therapy

Plaster me to a harness and send me away. Pull me up by my intestines and Bing! But how long? It could be a ditty about love (no you can not say that) and menses.

How do we decide on the favorites? In some fashioned molecule we know which dog to buy and to bury.

Remain vigilant, Hester. Cast a ceiling tile over your re-growth and see the days of your room.

        I am a room. I sit in the conspicuous loneliness.

Laika

means "barker" in Russian and we have a Bob Barker
from The Price is Right—
you could have watched as a child,
seen Bob Barker give money to PETA and support
spaying and neutering your pet. He donated
money to SHARK, and writes letters to legislators,
keeps a revolver next to his bed
It's perfectly all right to have a revolver by my bed.
If someone is prepared to attack me, I'm prepared to defend
myself. I don't need an assault weapon for that.
I'm a pretty good shot.

Canine Astronomy Lesson

Where, when it shrieks, horticulture mixes us

an ordinary gun? Under the greatest cells, is Nam
        starker than day. Then what shone right

all but shrieked for themselves—answering, conveniently,
        and her be wondering as so, while this jealous and terse cage

leaves your youth door—and, fine yams and Rhine, when they go East
        sweetly, until the halt is flipped under, and lucky it is to be

        locked-up.

The Cage and the Animal

They can fly up there,

dogs and wrens,

they can fill a short breeze and take it all
the way until they are boosted out of the atmosphere--

We have traded liturgy homily barley derriere pessimist genocide

love martyrdom massacre heaven solitude mortar pestle

friction gallant burnish champion race calibrate masturbate

flagellate garnish consume beckon embellish fatal

Earth capsule sky fire asphyxiate starve learn

repeat.   Repeat.

Hester's Wish

Stand up broken. Send some silly subhuman to a dam and open it up. Powerlessness has consequences, has opened up. Let's run.

But who is so fugacious? There is no transitory opposition. We are all running toward the dam, and then, running from it. We are only power in the end stop. Don't you see, Hester? There is no pan flute. These are just words too. Just a breathing.

> Beat, little sweet heart.

In the basted monolith of demolition we all have something to say. Stand out precious. I want that to be mine. We are not arguing, we are just mean and lovely. But, maybe we should argue? Who has dictated a sedation?

> Bend, salient love.

And still, this year our infrastructure is barely dust. Why is the second childhood so over analyzed? How solid and ironed it used to be. Deep, deep, influx of innocence. Haven't you done it to us already?

> Borrow causal time.

Stiff and flagrant celebrating—a rapine. Doom, doom, the herding and blustering of our lives. We are becoming to sheer. Watch your mouth! Watch everything you say. There is a hawking of our souls. Look West.

> Haze in the sun.

We are splitting. There are two of us Hester. A head-dress. And I cannot define anything. Sweet sun, pull your challenged comfort over my head. Let's sit and discuss how it was. I want it all back. I am the annals of the subconscious. I am the malady of error itself.

> Brilliant care.

Dog

You cannot thrust me into the abyss; you or you or you, a blind commodore or marooned character. No sail to Ephesus or Rome can kill the fade that rims my eyelids now, purple and raised and yet of merit. I will not presume you and your gristle will even discuss the goodhearted and golden things of life, the gardens and prayer rugs.

We will likely see each other again, similar to a log jam or Millay and her lover on her way to the mingling of liberation, goofballs, and ecstasy. You and your filigrees can finagle the fire-escape of life, a twisting, and undulating static while I volley the Midwest out of you.

[annals: show]

I am half-broken
an annex of frequency

I told you the shit
would hit the fan

we sang too much
at the midnight show

no medicine now
just calamity

[annals: concede]

what humanitarian
is this—mollified

or consumptive
I am a helpmate

I concede
what's that

sheets and sheets
billboards and billboards

[annals: rake]

be sanctity!
be light

be omen
or adjurn

so concise
what rake

what oryx
take me with you

[annals: tag]

I am chosen
cast to butte

hill master
no mistress

who's auxiliary
light has been

tagged
crated in cold

[annals: foster]

different quake
I look up   or out

there is no agony
just again and again

the shrinking
the shoemaker

foster
intransitive

[annals: catch]

now beauty
(what's this, loot)

soot, or toot
what root

my foot
your cut

we catch
we catch

[annals: lift]

dirty earth
dirty apes

dirty space
dirty waste

dirty caste
dirty shift

dirty lift
lift, lift

                        off

[annals: evolve]

sin and din
remarkable bed bug

fatted bang
sin and rang

solve
vent and resolve

I am roiling
I am sin

[annals: thrust]

under the stars
we locate the most

ordinary bitch
(celsius, certified)

and take her life
that is all

The Hoohah

Dear lullaby, you are not working,
not consoling those red mountains
fulcrum at night.
Proceed, switching to decaf.

There's going to be a molded nation here. A cambium of proportion
for the viewed.
Let her go. Let her smell her work.

Dear mastectomy,
you are not providing any relief when it comes to emoticons
(we are not being irreverent).
When filing down the halls and wings of the hoohah.
Hoooohaaaaaaaaaah.

Letter me back. Pry nonce. Sell, sell, sell.

Foliation as Girl

Girl as hawk,

{   }

Hawk landing on   {

Man   }

Frequency!

Stampeding of Horses and Feet

And to listen to the ways we all drink. The pre-eminent swirl of glisten on our tongues–you will grow and power the wagon, the mentioned air of title-hood. Why are we complaining? We said we would be happy if we ate one more. We hand you the bitten outright.

There are many omens here: a few days of a grasshopper, hawk eating snake. The water forms a halter and the pipe curves around Lucy—she is a pony. We are dead, she said. We have never been alive.

I look over and see your pale hair bobbing up and down with confidence and agree that we all need to speak.

Dr. Malashenkov

        has now revealed several new details

              about Laika's mission,

      such as her food being in jelly form

she was chained to prevent her turning

    around.

There was a carbon dioxide absorbing

           device in the cabin

                  to prevent the accumulation of

this toxic

        gas, as well as an oxygen generator.

A fan was automatically activated to keep the dog

    cool when the capsule's temperature

exceeded 15 degrees Celsius.

        According to Dr. Malashenkov, a great

deal of work

                            had to be done

                  to adapt a group of dogs to the conditions

in the tight cabin .

They were kept in gradually smaller cages

        periods up to 15-20 days.

Three dogs were trained for the Sputnik 2 flight:

                Albina,

                      Laika and Mushka.

        Albina was the first

    "backup".

[from *BBC News World Edition]

Albina & Mushka

Downcast and dour, no what birds!
        Illicit though once scouring
some cobbles and mash-hands,
        or snow-curds,
full now in cages and out of body.

Out of the world of rebirth —
        parlor to parlor, then sound to sound
waiting to be launched.
        Parfaits for the space race

o, what tilt! The clear management
        of the beast, metal timber
glass pockets, straps and instrumentation.
        Calories for hungry programs

those dogs, bounty. Bare. Befouled.

Voices of the Airways

Does that tear in the universal tape scare you like it does me? When we are transported to horsewoman-hood? This is where beelines steal your soul, like you are hidden under their equilibrium ironclad. Strings hang us on the infinite caravan. Our head is eyesight amongst the blue grass and fiddles.

Horse Well

Up from the horse well I climb. The calibrated
toil lines my fingernails, smell of must
and bee sting is bleached away. The tremulous
trunks are scrubbed bare and leaves are diced for dinner,
or consumption, my skin peels in horror.
My muscles are intestines that have traversed
despair and too much artificial light.
There is a polishing of wires and spires.
The undulating lines at the precipice
Sing the shape of a horse's head—cold blood,
Irish Draught. There is no teaching without learning,
No homo sapien without heart.
Just the head and tail of the serpent.

Horse Well

Up from the hoosegow I climb. The calibrated
toil lines my fishwife, smell of must
and bee sting is burnished away. The tremulous
trunks are scrubbed bare and lanyards are diced for dinner,
or consumption, my sixthsense peels in horror.
My muscles are inbreedings that have traversed
despair and too much auriculate light.
There is a polishing of wrinkles and spires.
The undulating lobes at the precipice
sing the shape of a heriot's head—cold blood,
Irish Draught. There is no thaneship without learning,
no homo sapien without Herrod.
Just the head and toil of the serpent.

Horse Well

Up from the hologram I climb. The calibrated
toil lines my festoonery, as the smell of must
and bee sting is brewed away. The tremulous
trunks are scrubbed bare and larches are diced for dinner,
as consumption, my sidearm, peels in horror.
My muscles are invocations that have traversed
despair and too much anointed light.
There is a polishing of willynilly and spires.
The undulating lodestone at the precipice
sings the shape of a holy roller's head—cold blood,
Irish Draught. There is no tea garden without learning,
no homo sapien without hogwash.
Just the head and talisman of the serpent.

Horse Well

Up from the Holy Saturday I climb. The calibrated
toil lines my fertility, smell of must
and bee sting is bused away. The tremulous
trunks are scrubbed bare and Lilliputians are diced for dinner,
or consumption, my senility peels in horror.
My muscles are idiot boxes that have traversed
despair and too much amphibious light.
There is a polishing of wanigan and spires.
The undulating linguistics at the precipice
sing the shape of a hem's head—cold blood,
Irish Draught. There is no thumbscrew without learning,
no homo sapien without hegemony.
Just the head and tattoo of the serpent.

Horse Well

Up from the harness race I climb. The calibrated
toil lines my freckles, smell of must
and bee sting is burrowed away. The tremulous
trunks are scrubbed bare and limelight is diced for dinner,
or consumption, synonyms peels in horror.
My muscles are imprints that have traversed
despair and too much argentine light.
There is a polishing of wampum and spires.
The undulating ladderbacks at the precipice
sing the shape of a hound's head—cold blood,
Irish Draught. There is no Time without learning,
no homo sapien without Heart.
Just the head and tongue of the serpent.

Semantics

We went bowling that day. Me, Dandelion,
and Alf. We walked up the plank after Alf
got a strike— Dandelion wanted to jump
ship. I suggested he try a free trial of Paxil for
his social anxiety disorder. In the distance was a sail
connected to a bottle of mineral water, the expensive
French kind. Alf and I felt like martyrs when we used
that old gaff to pick up the sail. We laughed at a scene in Moby Dick
and sat arguing about the pronunciation of quahog.

"Why would Ishmael and Queequeg eat cod chowder
after they just ate quahog chowder?" Dandelion asked.
Alf and I laughed at his obsequious misconception
of chowder. The three of us sat down to begin counting
the kernals of corn that were delivered to us by Fed Ex
earlier that morning. "Maybe they were really hungry,"
Dandelion added. "Oh dandelion," I said,
"you're such a semiotician!"

breath

Re-memory of Water

feet are peeling.

        My life is treacherous.

Clothes are Roman.

My back is greeting you.

These are the values we discussed.

{   discussion   }

My eyes look black.

{   reflection   }

Follow the panhuman air.

{ transgression }

Hester's Shoes

How sweet phyton stands at your heels. We have talked of maladies in this light, and there is only a recognizable desire. Punish such immaturity and Zionize Manolos! I looked at the heels on that one or this one and decided only against the color.

Dear immoderate balancing act. Your weight cannot be held all the time by those. Sit and stitch with Manolo, watch him work, see his cold eyes, but pardon the fungi of too much use. Their only match is an apron (and no abortion).

      God says you will have that baby, baby.

How you write such saccharin letters! No fundamentalism, no weeping. Just a full grown house. But, we are ousted. It's funny that there is not talking or even e-mailing. We are leaving that place, that boutique for an ostracized mind. Not palatable, not semiotic. We have no language left, dear. Now charge and tie your best bow.

      Senescent being, you owe me.

Dear blaspheme, we preen our earth and natural holidays and yet there is still a silence. No theatre, no texture left to the movement. Dance for me. I will burn all my shoes if you dance for me.

      We are not talking about owing here.

This is all lessoned by the thread of all those shoes remaining unused on your floor. And there are so many left to buy. We are buried in our shoes, burned in our shoes, beaten in our shoes. But God is telling me that I can pass them down to the second wife, or even the third. No more babies, baby.

      We are not talking about owning here.

Some Women Marry Houses

My children weren't righteous. They stumbled because I was evil. They were doomed to perish in the fires of hell.
–Andrea Yates

I pray this bespattered nonsense comes to bear a certain tag. Useless, meaningful. Whatever it is, it is surely feminist. I wrote that word on Post-It notes and plastered them like a soliloquy. We played a game called how are you and I like your shoes.
Black, black, black this hollow mold holds a fishwife; such apostasy in that nation.

Sick, the bald notions of a child—late at night, you see a shade pillowing her head, or is it her head on a pillow? It was the seventh deadly sin.

We walked to hell to see what it was like and we decided we liked it better than the universe. There were no more secret conversations between women about women. No Greek salads and flushed senseless tragedies. We walked to Montenegro and balanced the corks of our Diet Cokes on our noses. Seals: hooting and woofing, clapping and banding together.

Swooped in were more women in coats of felt and fakery. But nothing compared to the sweetness of anti-psychotics and hormones—facile and grand.

Swimmer's Ear

He said marriage is a cage. I want to put my head down without a roach or without a bargain. I want to masturbate during prayer, skim the major works, and drive ten hours straight in a diaper. He said he went to West Virginia. It went like this:

I didn't go to New York.

I went to West Virginia.

You don't know shit.

Go to hell.

We are all sickened by the morphing of our inner ears. We are all susceptible to the compromising and re-styling of our hyenas.

Laika's Rendezvous

I've forgiven you. I've forgiven the second-day star, and the one after that.

Today an angel visited me. She told me that she loves me

and that when I die, something will come of my death.

She told me that beyond this universe is another, where I will appear again.

And again, and will never die.

My God.

Mountains of Brie and Wiry Ocean

Dear Spiral,

How do you keep your circle of life in such a rambling monotone? What part of was was? If I could paint you a picture of tutelage and Romulus, I would. But, alas, vamped!

                (fuck the middle man)

We shall end up in the love of quilts and dharma and that shit will remain.

                (cursed summer!)

Shunyata

Shunyata

Shunyata.

Neutral happens ultimate being.   Salivate   priestly capital Vonage!

Dog

My unceremonious catastrophe. The way you licked me clean with your swollen tongue and useless rage.

But we are all in the same place. Physical characteristics so heightened by a dope star. The window is down, it is raining. I cannot get the window up again.

And a pallid suspect is sitting in my house remembering the visions of trips and unbelief that fasten my existence. In-depth, in a turnstile.

Cadence that is an imbalance of light—I fall off of you, onto the hard wet makeshift ground. We cannot ask any more questions. It is time to sit and recite my breached dream; wholly disheartened, wholly alive.

I will launch disaster upon you, delineate our simple thread until the night leaves my consciousness.

Hester's Rampage

My life is measured by cubits! I have five minutes to send a rage your way, and no we are not minimizing the rats or even the rafters. Can we deal with the plummeting salutations of our age? Let us become mighty. We are not in Rome and I am not a genius, a Romberg or Schopenhauer. There is a mile post here. Don't ignore it you will be set on fire! Only residually and resiliently can I become the motion or a past experience. I want to sleep all night but no one does. I want to run away from the dirty dead fools and play the organ. Can't you come with me? That golden urn—turn it over! That layman, tell him good bye. We feel what is between our legs and beneath our bones. There is no sending of laws. No, just the sick smell of the morning.

Hester

Look toward the freezing salience of rain. Your mouth enters mine and the torrent is on. A fancy, windswept concubine that dances with God. My sway is so lucid and variant I fancy something new. You fill me, entering the recesses like a recluse. There is the same and the same and the same. No floating in salt.

The glummest of epiphanies: I am not dying, not telling myself anything. Only the infirm and undulating mummies can retire this way. The humanity is retracted and calcified.

All girls are born into the dynasty of the arachnid. A sack of possibility and fire, the long spaces theirs for the taking.

Planet Hester

A whimpering in this suite says go on. We watch our lives drift into plastic and someone yells wait, that's a boat!

What have you reconciled? What have you conformed in these hours of clicking and running and fighting? My name begins with a short hop. My friend's name starts with pancakes that are bitter.

If we circle ourselves up high, in those heavens, what will come of it? I was once a dog and fueled myself with myself. I remember the last hours of it, a slight choke and then,

                    Heaven, chocolate angels,

I can't begin to tell you how the dog dies. The coughing of blood, the groan, the wasting. We have not wasted this bread loaf on him. She is courteous and dogs and spiders remain my weaknesses. They will always be and begin and hold.

Sweet pie. The monstrous orbs and lights (what aliens?) are salivating at the inadvertent coupling. Such coarsening. Damned pecans of doom and reticence. My syruped intentions are too great.

Star

The meaning of a name could be a grocery store rag
never left the shelf like crumble like blue compost
what can't we recant

to a star

confess to a paper

sing to a girl

destroy

and lick it up again.

Terrible

Underthings, like cats, are impassible. Their rid, their autopsy, is too grandiose for these stars. I am dying and no breath of the future will pass through my window.

What a copper border that is ensconced around the Earth. And, there is no autumn here. I am a dog. An inchworm. An ingenue.

Match, match, match the sentences of darkness to each other until they preserve, or thumb back at the wretch.

Cowpuncher

I ride to your fescue—it creeps along the doors, brass cracks, and plagued indifference like a cascade. I roam valleys of good intentions and majesty with hopes that your deal is due to my asking. I sit rocking, trying not to undersell the years of baking and cooking. A vestibule, my knees are worn, yet I need them to move on.

[annals: see]

fillagreed chicory as bright as a bore

this pasteurized universe

has planed me

dynamite

here's the kicker

like a barfly or a banshee

I am not leaving I like it like neon

[annals: crill]

foul men and chimes
are gone like a joke

the sea is abundant
situated warmth

and crill!
pendulous points

beacons of fluorescence
what otherwise is invisible

[annals: oceans]

otherworldly to oceans
perhaps a rocket

to space
the rubric of death

my bower
my bonus sounds

full of bones
full of bones

[annals: argent]

ruffle, ruffle
artificial

homicide   silver sky
porous we

make ourselves
determinant

leave me
leave me

[annals: autosuggestion]

hester has left the building
hester has left the building

hester has baked a cake
hester has baked a cake

hester has put on a dress
hester has put on a dress

hester has become a ceo
hester has become a ceo

hester has gotten married
hester has gotten married

hester celebrated easter
hester celebrated easter

hester divorced
hester divorced

hester got a rescue dog
hester got a rescue dog

hester lived in new York city
hester lived in new York city

hester rode the train
hester rode the train

hester got robbed
hester got robbed

hester filed a report
hester filed a report

hester was told to be more careful
hester was told to be more careful

hester went home
hester went home

Guarantor

We have come to know the bellyaching as good. We have come to see the teeth falling out of our mouths—the oiled and limp birds, floating in the dark. Where does all the trash go? Where are yesterday's carcasses? What should I eat for breakfast?

    (The nasty solitude that sits in my mouth like semen.)

And then, filed in, is triumph; horses a mile long. I want them as far as I can hear, gray and dappled—muddy and fly-eaten. One wades his nose through a large horn of weeds and stops to notice a dragonfly. I recognize the nucleus of the moment, hot and barely breathing.

I am fastened by a halter to a fence. I would like to eat some grass.

Average

I reap the Appalachian foothills where Scott Joplin sings life into moths. I chill in the rustic low song of bird and katydid. It is wet in my throat and my gums spake nothing. Two woodpeckers. Two red heads. They are the same, not different.

We sit and feel the weight of our years together. A burning, a bust, a born-again limb. You are like pommes frites, a shot of frantic, a bloom of the inevitable. We will try, together, to maintain that path to the sun. In all of its humor.

Remarkable

Wash your hands. Wash the philosophical list from your legs, your arms. These are the wing nuts we have asked for. I am supposed to work with them.

Pithy ramble: voice, newspaper and polyglot. Flee from me. (Hold me down. Hold me accountable.)

It is an argument for spring. And who needs to argue? Over a cold beer, a lit cigarette, a beautifully tanned woman.

Plagued is the listlessness. So heavy it pulls at the hem of a cool dress. So wretched—

There is a stream at the end of the road—a meeting of bridge and black cat, where the water, the white clay is filled with glass and tadpoles. But this is too long to be narration, too frayed to hold a story.

So we sit and immortalize the birds. (Again.)

We sit and remember the red fox dead on the highway margin. And we say: let go red fox. Ride the pale air.

NOTES

Many of the poems in the manuscript reference Laika, the first dog in space, who went up in Sputnik II in 1957. Animal rights groups were appalled. Laika's life in space is not known exactly, but it is believed dog died of either asphyxiation or sheer trauma at take off.

Many of the poems reference a "Hester", which may or may not be Hawthorne's Hester Prynne—or may or may not be Esther from the The Old Testament.

The italicized portions in the poem, Laika, have been taken from Time Swampland, February 5, 2013 edition.

"Horse Well" (all five) are obviously renditions of the same poem with different words inserted in the same places. Similar to Oulipo's N+7; however, the words I chose to replace are not all nouns, were selected at random, and although the dictionary was used to replace the deleted words, there was no specific mathematical count. The horse well is derived from lore of Pegasus, the winged horse, drinking from the well of Pirene.

"Canine Astronomy Lesson" is a homophonic translation of the original German of one of Rilke's Sonnets to Orpheus.

"Stampeding of Horses and Feet" is a line from Carole Maso's AVA.

"The Cage and the Animal" is taken from the title of a text by the same name by Donald Hall.

"Some Women Marry Houses" is borrowed from the Anne Sexton poem of the same name.

Kristine Snodgrass is the author of *The War on Pants* from Jack Leg Press, and co-author of the collaboration *Two Thieves and a Liar* with Neil De La Flor and Maureen Seaton. She is Co-director of Anhinga Press and teaches in the Department of English and Modern Languages at Florida Agricultural and Mechanical University in Tallahassee, FL.

www.ingramcontent.com/pod-product-compliance
Lightning Source LLC
Chambersburg PA
CBHW052029290426
44112CB00014B/2440